Earth's Changing Coasts

by Neil Morris

www.raintreepublishers.co.uk

Visit our website to find out more information about **Raintree** books.

To order:

 Phone 44 (0) 1865 888112

Send a fax to 44 (0) 1865 314091

 Visit the Raintree Bookshop at **www.raintreepublishers.co.uk** to browse our catalogue and order online.

First published in Great Britain by Raintree, Halley Court, Jordan Hill, Oxford OX2 8EJ, part of Harcourt Education.
Raintree is a registered trademark of Harcourt Education Ltd.

Editorial: Nick Hunter and Catherine Clarke
Design: Michelle Lisseter and Bridge Creative Services Ltd
Picture Research: Maria Joannou and Liz Eddison
Illustrations: Bridge Creative Services Ltd
Production: Jonathan Smith

Originated by Dot Gradations Ltd
Printed and bound in China by South China Printing Company

ISBN 1 844 21392 7 (hardback)
07 06 05 04 03
10 9 8 7 6 5 4 3 2 1

ISBN 1 844 21399 4 (paperback)
08 07 06 05 04
10 9 8 7 6 5 4 3 2 1

British Library Cataloguing in Publication Data
Morris, Neil
Earth's Changing Coasts. – (Landscapes and People)
551.4'57
A full catalogue record for this book is available from the British Library.

Acknowledgements
The publishers would like to thank the following for permission to reproduce photographs:
Bruce Coleman Collection pp. 9, 15 (Jeff Foott), 20 (Judith Clark), 27 (Pacific Stock), Corbis pp. 4 (Neil Rabinowitz), 7 (Paul A. Souders), 8 (Chris North/Cordaiy Picture Library), 10 (Andrew Brown/Ecoscene), 11 (John Farmar; Cordaiy Photo Library Ltd), 14 (Gallo Images), 19 (Bettmann), 26 (Anthony Cooper); Getty Images pp. 13 (Stone), 21 (Imagebank), 22 (Taxi), 28 (Imagebank); National Oceanic and Atmospheric Administration p. 29; NHPA pp. 16 (John Shaw), 17 (Alan Williams), 24 (Daniel Heuclin); Oxford Scientific Films (Martyn Chillmaid) p. 6.

Cover photograph of Rio de Janeiro reproduced with permission of Corbis (Wolfgang Kaehler).

The publishers would like to thank Margaret Mackintosh for her assistance in the preparation of this book.

Every effort has been made to contact copyright holders of any material reproduced in this book. Any omissions will be rectified in subsequent printings if notice is given to the publishers.

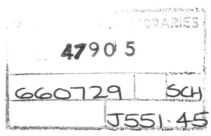

Contents

Any words appearing in the text in bold, **like this**, are explained in the Glossary.

What is a coast?

What do you think of when you think of the coast? Does it have sandy beaches, palm trees and warm blue seas? Does it have high, rocky **cliffs**? Or perhaps it has a busy **harbour** with fishing boats and sailing yachts? Whichever one you think of, you're right. The coast can be all of these things, and many others too.

More than two-thirds of Earth's surface is covered by oceans and seas. This means that land makes up less than one-third of the surface of Earth. What we call the coast is the place where the sea meets the land.

The line of the coast is rarely straight, as this Caribbean shoreline shows. Beaches and bays are usually curved, and their shape is constantly changing.

Around the world

All of the world's great land masses, called **continents**, are surrounded by sea and have long coastlines. There are seven continents – Africa, Antarctica, Asia, Europe, North America, South America and Oceania. Around these continents are four large oceans – the Pacific, Atlantic, Indian and Arctic oceans.

The world's coasts are constantly changing. Where the powerful force of the sea meets the land, waves pound against the **shore** and gradually wear away at rocks. The waves break off pieces of rock and eventually lay them down somewhere else as dunes or beaches. This changes the shape of our coasts.

Looking at coasts

In this book we look at many different kinds of coasts. We see how they were formed and how they have changed over the years. We look at the animals and plants that live along the coastline and the ways in which people living beside coasts use and change them.

This map shows the world's continents and oceans. The Southern Ocean, around the frozen continent of Antarctica, is made up of parts of three other oceans.

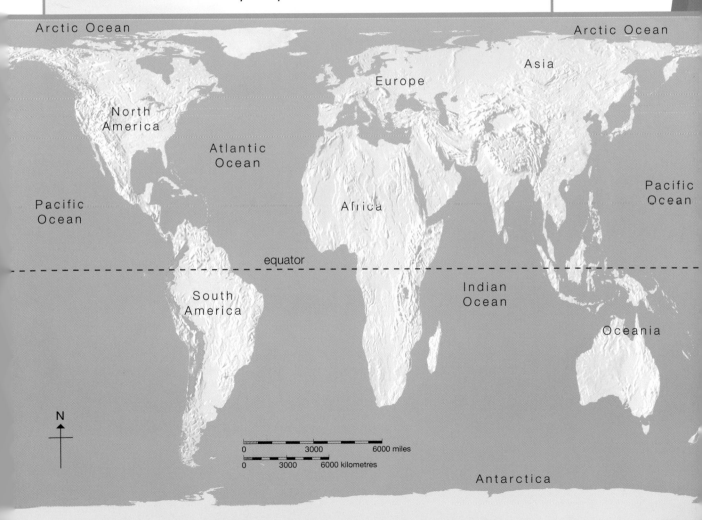

Arctic Ocean

Arctic Ocean

Asia

Europe

North America

Atlantic Ocean

Pacific Ocean

Pacific Ocean

Africa

equator

South America

Indian Ocean

Oceania

N

0   3000   6000 miles
0   3000   6000 kilometres

Antarctica

How do coasts form and change?

The action of the sea carves the shapes of the world's coastlines. There are many different kinds of coasts, which vary according to their location in the world. The **climate**, and especially the wind, has a great effect on the sea. The wind pushes the sea into waves, and in turn the movement of waves affects the coast.

Over many years, the pounding of waves can wear away even the hardest rocks.

Wave power

Waves are made by wind blowing over the sea. They may begin as tiny ripples, but by the time they reach the coast, waves can be large and powerful. As a large wave gets near to the **shore**, where the sea is shallow, its top curves and makes frothy foam called surf. This is a breaking wave, or **breaker**. Breakers move fast and have enormous power. As they hit land, they throw tonnes of foaming water against the shore.

Wearing away

Water is heavy, so when it moves fast, it has great force. This is why waves gradually wear away rocks, in a process called **erosion**. Some rocks are harder than others, and this hardness makes a difference to the effects of erosion. **Cliffs** made of softer rock, such as **chalk**, are worn away more quickly than harder rock such as **granite**. Chalk cliffs crumble away, especially during storms. With harder rock, water and air bubbles are forced into tiny cracks when a wave hits. They squash the air in the cracks, like a hammer driving a wedge. This process weakens the rocks, so that eventually bits break off and fall into the sea.

As foaming water rushes in and out of cracks in cliffs, day after day, year after year, rocks begin to break up.

Destructive waves

The biggest, most powerful waves are called **tsunamis** (from the Japanese words meaning '**harbour** waves'). A tsunami can move at up to 800 kilometres (497 miles) an hour in the open sea. It can reach heights of more than 30 metres by the time it gets to the shore. Such giant waves are sometimes called tidal waves, but they have nothing to do with tides. They are actually caused by **earthquakes** under the **seabed**. When an earthquake shakes under the sea, it makes waves that race across the ocean. Tsunamis can cause great damage to coasts, throwing rocks on to the shore, washing beaches away and destroying harbours and houses. Fortunately for people living by the coast, these enormous waves are rare.

Different coastal landscapes

Where the land meets the sea, different kinds of rocks cause different shapes of coasts. Very often there are hard and soft rocks along the same piece of coast. Over a period of time, soft rocks are worn away, while hard rocks are able to withstand the sea for longer. This creates a coast with **bays** and **headlands**. The bays are formed in the soft rock, and the headlands are made up of harder rock.

> *Lulworth Cove, on the southern coast of England, forms an almost perfect circle.*

Bays and circular coves

Rocks are formed in layers, called **strata**. Where layers of soft rock are exposed to the sea, wide curving bays are formed. Smaller bays are called **coves**. These occur when the sea finds a small weak spot in a **cliff** and forces its way through. This forms a tiny cove, which gets larger as the sea swirls into it and wears away its sides. Over a long period of time, this can make a circular cove.

Caves, arches and stacks

Waves can cut out a small hollow in a cliff face. The pounding action of the waves can make the hollow bigger and bigger, until it becomes a cave. Sometimes holes are made in the roof of the cave, where water forces its way up. These are known as blowholes. When caves break right through a headland, or two caves meet back to back, they can form an arch. When this happens, the roof of the arch gradually gets worn away and eventually falls down. This leaves one wall of the arch standing as a stack.

These limestone stacks once formed part of the coastal cliffs. They are part of a group called the Twelve Apostles that stand near Port Campbell in south-east Australia.

Changes over time

Many coastal changes take place over a very long time. It may take hundreds or even thousands of years for a cave to be formed by pounding waves, for example. The process might speed up if there are changes in **climate**, such as stormy weather, and when the roof of an arch collapses – the action may all be over in a few seconds. Geologists study rocks and their strata to build up a picture of Earth's past. To them, a thousand years is a short period of geological time. Because of this, the way in which rocks are exposed and broken down at the coast is very useful to them.

Beaches

A beach is a strip of land that slopes gently down to the sea. Beaches begin forming when waves wear away **cliffs**. Large pieces of rock break off and crash down to the ground below. There, they are pounded by waves and broken down into smaller pieces. In this way large **boulders** are eventually turned into small pebbles. The action of the waves makes pebbles smooth and shiny. In stormy weather, the pebbles are thrown back up the slope of the beach, causing more **erosion**. This further wearing-away process is called **abrasion**.

The wind often blows sand to the back of a beach. There it can pile up to make sand dunes. These move constantly, changing shape according to wind and weather.

From pebbles to sand

On many beaches, pebbles are worn down to the very tiny grains that we call sand. The colour and texture of the sand depends on the type of rocks from which it is made. Most sand is a yellowish colour – the 'golden sands' you may read about in holiday brochures. This is made of grains of quartz, a **mineral** found in many different types of rock. Some tropical beaches are made mainly of tiny pieces of broken seashells and **coral**, rather than rock. These beaches have fine white sand. Other beaches are made up of small grains of **volcanic rock**, and these sometimes make black sand.

Moving sand

As well as moving up and down a beach, from the edge of the sea to the land, small pebbles (called shingle) and sand move along the beach too. This is because waves rarely break straight on to a beach, but strike it at an angle. As they do so, the waves push the sand along the beach, in a process called longshore drift. The sand drifts along the **shore**. Sometimes the drifting sand then forms a **bar**, or **spit**. These move and change all the time.

Hurst Castle stands on this 2 mile spit, stretching out into the English Channel. In the hundreds of years since the castle was built, the shape of this spit has probably changed.

Sogne Fjord

Fjords

More than 10,000 years ago, during the last **ice age**, **glaciers** covered northern Europe and North America. These slow-moving rivers of ice carved out deep, steep-sided **valleys**. When the ice age ended and large parts of a huge ice sheet started to

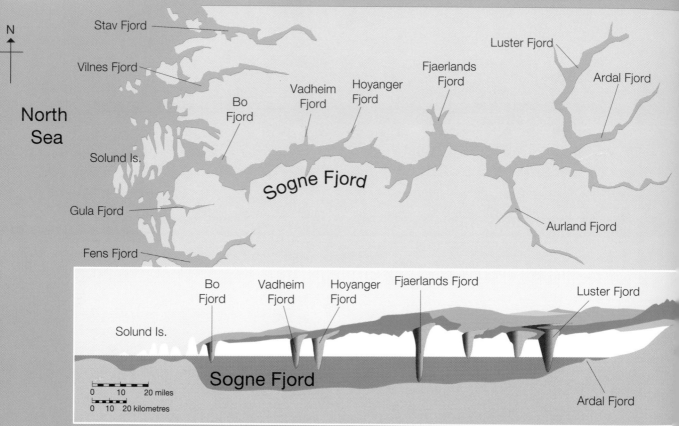

King of the Fjords

King of the Fjords

Fjord comes from a Norwegian word, and it is in Norway that we find some of the world's longest and deepest examples. Sogne Fjord is just one of more than 200 large fjords that cut into the west coast of Norway. It stretches inland for 204 kilometres (127 miles) and is known as the 'King of the Fjords'. Sogne Fjord is more than 5 kilometres (3 miles) across at its widest point. Scientists believe that its valleys were first formed by rivers flowing through them about 50 million years ago. As its ice melts, the nearby Jostedal Glacier still feeds the *fjord* with water.

melt, the extra water made the sea level rise. The glaciers also started to melt, and their valleys filled with water. The flooded valleys formed long, deep **inlets** that we call **fjords**.

Sounds and estuaries

There are many fjords in northern North America. In Alaska and the Canadian province of British Columbia, they are often called sounds. Along the coast of South Island in New Zealand, there is a national park named Fjordland. Its biggest fjord is called Milford Sound. In other, warmer parts of the world, drowned valleys formed estuaries along the coast. These estuaries are the wide mouths of rivers, which flooded when sea levels rose after the last ice age.

These canoers are resting on the still waters of the Kenai Fjord, Alaska, USA, enjoying the beautiful landscape around them.

Daily changes

Many coasts change every day. This is because the water in seas and oceans moves around in tides. Tides usually rise and fall twice a day. When the tide is high, more of the coast is covered by water. At the same time, the tide is low somewhere else. You can see the difference between high and low tide on a beach with a shallow slope. Although the water level may only rise a few metres, a wide area of sand at low tide can become a very narrow beach at high tide.

Life near the water's edge

Millions of creatures live in the sea, and many other animals like to live near the coast. They make their homes on the **shore**, where it is easy for them to catch fish and other **marine animals** for food. The lives of many coastal animals change with the seasons, especially those that live where it is very hot in summer or very cold in winter. The penguins of the frozen Antarctic region, for example, must move further north in winter to reach the edge of the ice and dive in the sea to catch fish.

This colony of seals is on the coast of southern Africa. Seals are very good swimmers and catch all their food in the sea.

Coastal waters

Many kinds of fish and other marine animals spend their whole lives in shallow coastal waters. There are some flowering plants in this region and many different kinds of seaweed. In stormy weather, seaweeds are sometimes torn away from their rocks and flung up the beach. They are tough, rubbery plants, however, and this helps them live in and out of the water.

*Fiddler crabs like this one live on muddy shorelines in warm **climates**.*

Wading in the shallows

Wading birds spend a great deal of time on the seashore, wandering about in the shallows looking for small sea creatures to eat. All waders have long legs, so that their bodies are out of the water, and most have long, stabbing beaks. The oystercatcher is a good example. It lives on rocky shores and sandy beaches, catching and eating small crabs, worms and mussels. It can break **shellfish** open with its strong beak.

Between the tides

On the seashore there is an area of rock, pebbles and sand which changes twice a day with the tides. This intertidal area (area between the tides) is exposed at low tide and covered by the sea at high tide. This part of the seashore is teeming with animals and plants. Some, such as crabs, are able to live both in and out of water, which gives them a great advantage. Crabs eat small animals and the remains of dead creatures. They grasp food with their strong pincers. Crabs that live in burrows beneath the **waterline** at high tide, such as fiddler crabs, hide away there when the tide is in. This keeps them safe from **predators**.

Intertidal zones

The intertidal area can be divided into four zones: lower, middle and upper **shore**, and the splash zone. Each zone has its own kind of life and constantly changes with the tides. The lower shore (near the low-tide mark) is covered by sea most of the time. Shrimps, snails and tubeworms live there, as well as many small fish. Further up the slope of the beach, the middle shore is exposed to the air twice a day for a few hours. This is home to **sea anemones**, mussels and sea urchins. Barnacles, periwinkles and crabs live on the upper shore. Finally, just above the high-tide mark, is the splash zone. Small winkles and sandhoppers have made this region of sea spray their home.

Rock pools

Some coasts have a level area of rock at the base of cliffs, called a wave-cut platform (because it is carved out by waves). Very often there are holes in the platform, and water is left there when the tide goes out. We call these holes rock pools, and they are a difficult place for animals to live because of the tide constantly coming in and going out. Nevertheless, some small fish, shrimps and crabs have **adapted** to this life of constant change. Rock pools are a good place to observe small wildlife in action, but make sure you watch out for the tide coming in!

This puffin's beak is full of sand eels it has caught to feed its chicks.

At home by the sea

Many kinds of sea birds make their nests on **cliffs** high above the seashore. They crowd together in huge **colonies**. This makes them feel safe from much larger birds such as the peregrine falcon. Sea birds don't need much space on land, because they do all their feeding at sea. Fulmars nest on cliff ledges, and parents catch most of the fish they need to feed their young by swimming on the surface of the water. Gannets also nest on cliffs, but they fish in a different way – flying down from a great height and diving into the sea to catch their food.

On top of the cliffs

Puffins also live in large groups. They nest in burrows at the top of cliffs. As with other sea birds, the most important thing about the location of the nest is food. Puffins regularly dive into the sea, to catch small fish underwater.

17

Changing settlements

As early humans spread around the world more than 100,000 years ago, they learned to catch fish for food. Many of them followed coastlines so that they would never be short of a source of food. When they decided to stay in one place, these people built **settlements** near the seashore. These coastal people then became sailors, so that they could move around more easily.

People of the purple dye

The Phoenicians settled along the coast of the eastern Mediterranean some time before 1000 BC. There they built great city ports, such as Byblos, along the coast of present-day Lebanon. They were expert sailors and began trading along the coast of North Africa. They usually sailed within sight of the coast, so that they knew where they

Phoenicians from Tyre founded the city of Carthage around 814 BC. From there they sailed to the islands of Sicily and Sardinia.

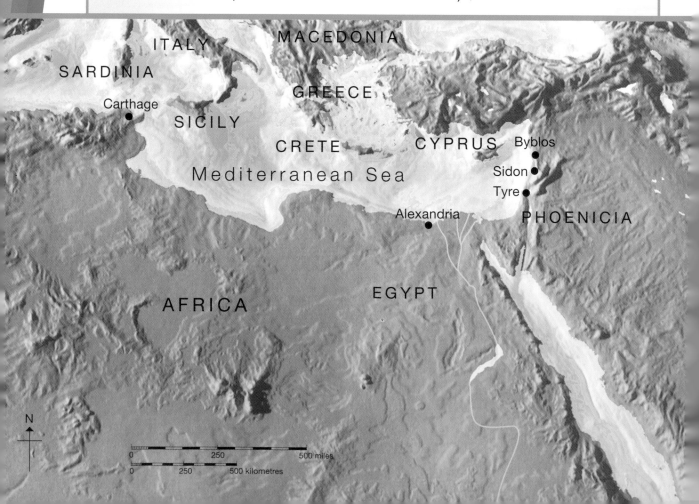

were and could land in stormy weather. They founded great ports, such as Carthage, building **harbours** in sheltered spots. One of the Phoenicians' specialities was a purple cloth, which they made by using a dye that came from the murex **shellfish** that they caught.

Port of Alexandria

In 332 BC Alexander the Great, the king of the Macedonians, captured the Phoenician coast before moving on to Egypt. There he founded a great port, which was named after him. Alexandria was near the mouth of the River Nile, and it grew into an important city on the Mediterranean coast. Alexander's workmen dredged up rocks and mud to build a **breakwater** between the city and a small island. The world's first lighthouse was built on the island, around 280 BC, to guide ships safely past rocks and into the narrow entrance of the harbour. It was listed among the Seven Wonders of the Ancient World.

The first fleet

Many coastal regions of the world were chosen simply because this was where people first arrived by sea. They were usually places with good, deep harbours. People first settled in Australia many thousands of years ago – Aborigines, who sailed there from south-east Asia. In 1788 a fleet of eleven ships from England arrived on the Australian coast. Captain Arthur Phillip (shown in the picture – right) commanded this fleet. They formed a **colony** beside a natural deep-water harbour, which grew into the city of Sydney. Today, there are almost 4 million people living in Sydney – about one in every five Australians lives in the coastal city.

Protecting settlements

During the 16th and 17th centuries, many European explorers sailed off to find new lands. Those who went with them used sheltered **bays** to set up **colonies**. People soon found that coasts could be dangerous places in stormy weather. They also realized that natural forces change beaches, and even **cliff** faces. So people began to protect their **harbours** and **settlements**. They started by building high sea walls, which protected them from floods and storm damage. As ships developed and got bigger, the harbours also needed to be larger and deeper.

Breaking waves

In more recent times, people started to build strong fences on beaches, at a right angle to the sea. These fences are called **groynes**. They break up the waves as they hit the **shore**. Just as important, they hold sand and pebbles in place, stopping them being washed along the beach by longshore drift (see page 11). Larger **breakwaters** are made of concrete and are sometimes built right out into the sea. They break up the force of the waves before they reach the shore. These are particularly useful for protecting harbours.

These groynes are dividing up a beach on the south coast of England. The tide was in when this photo was taken.

Soaking up energy

People have found that piles of big, heavy **boulders** can help to protect coastal towns from the effects of the sea. The waves' powerful energy is used up on the boulders, rather than cliffs or beaches. In recent years, interlocking concrete shapes called tetrapods have replaced boulders. These are also big and heavy, so that the force of the waves cannot carry them away.

Sea walls and breakwaters help to protect boats in the harbour at St Tropez, in southern France.

Managing the coast

Most of these attempts to manage the coast and protect people from the effects of the sea are successful only for a short time. The defences usually have to be rebuilt regularly because of the incredible force of the sea. The defences also have an effect on the nearby coastline. If people reduce the power of waves along their bay, they may find that sea currents, tides and waves have more of an effect on bays further down the coast. Natural forces change coastlines, and when we try to fight these forces, we cause other changes.

Beach resorts

Holidaymakers enjoy being by the sea, where they can swim, sail and have fun on the beach. Coastlines can be changed dramatically by tourists, however, and this is most clearly seen in beach **resorts**. As a small village by the sea becomes popular, it attracts more people from the region, who come to the village for work. More building of hotels and restaurants takes place, so that even more tourists are attracted. Before long, a small fishing village may have become a large resort town. In the 1950s Benidorm, on the Spanish Costa Blanca (called the 'white coast' because of its beautiful beaches), was a small fishing village. By the 1980s, it was full of high-rise hotels. The more tourists there are, the more chance there is of **pollution** from litter and other waste. The more land that is used for building hotels and other tourist attractions, the less natural **habitat** there is for the area's wildlife.

Yucatán Peninsula

In the 1970s, planners saw a deserted sand **spit** off a small fishing village on the Caribbean shore of Mexico's Yucatán **Peninsula**. They decided to build a tourist resort there, and the result was Cancún. As the resort grew, with many high-rise hotels, many thousands of Yucatecans from the surrounding region moved to Cancún in search of work. The resort now has a permanent population of 400,000 and more than 2 million visitors arrive each year. Most fly from far away, landing at Cancún's international airport. This development has brought money and employment to a poor region. Unfortunately, however, many foreign visitors arrive on all-inclusive package holidays and spend little money outside their hotels.

The 'hotel zone' of Cancún, in Mexico, lies on a spit of land. It is full of hotels, shops and restaurants.

ALABAMA GEORGIA ATLANTIC OCEAN

• Pensacola

• Carrabelle

• Jacksonville
• St. Augustine

Daytona Beach •

Cape Canaveral •

FLORIDA

New Port Richey •
Tarpon Springs •
Clearwater • • Tampa
St. Petersburg

Lake
Okeechobee

West Palm Beach •

Sarasota •

Fort Myers •

Fort Lauderdale

Naples •

Miami •

Everglades National Park

Key Largo •

North America

Florida

GULF OF MEXICO

Key West •

Biscayne National Park

N

0   30   60 miles
0   30   60 kilometres

Bringing people to the coast

The US state of Florida has a coastline that is more than
2000 kilometres (1250 miles) long. Florida is a peninsula that stretches
down the Gulf of Mexico to the west and the Atlantic Ocean to the
east. When all its **bays**, **lagoons** and islands are included, Florida's
coastline is more than 13,000 kilometres (8125 miles) long. The warm
climate throughout the year makes the region very attractive to tourists.
The coastal city of Miami averages high temperatures of between
24 and 32 °Celsius. The climate means that visitors from around the
world are happy to visit Florida all year round.

Changing coasts

Increasingly, our coasts are being harmed and spoiled by **pollution**. Sometimes this pollution is caused by an accident, but very often the causes could be avoided. Beaches are easily polluted by harmful litter, **sewage** and oil spills.

Sewage

In some places human waste is pumped straight into the sea without being treated first. This untreated sewage can be washed up on the **shore** and become a **health hazard**. It can spread germs and poison fish and **shellfish** that are later eaten by people. People swimming in the sea cannot see the germs, so they have no idea that their health may be in danger. In many tourist **resorts**, authorities test the water on favourite beaches to make sure that it is safe to swim.

Litter

The coast can become littered in two ways – by land and from the sea. Not only does litter look ugly and messy, it can also be very dangerous. Broken glass can cut people, while plastic can-holders can strangle birds. A lot of our litter is made of plastic, which may take many years to rot. Always take your litter home with you when you visit the beach.

Oil spills

One of the greatest dangers to beaches is oil pollution. If a storm pushes an oil tanker against rocks and damages it, millions of litres of oil can be released. Some of the oil sinks and may be washed up on beaches years later. Some oil floats and forms an oil slick, which gets washed up on the shore. This sticky mess traps and kills birds and other **marine animals**. The worst coastal damage like this was caused in 1989 by the *Exxon Valdez* oil tanker. The ship ran aground on Bligh Reef, off the southern coast of Alaska. It spilled around 38,000 tonnes of oil, which polluted over 2000 kilometres (1300 miles) of coast. Hundreds of thousands of fish, birds and other sea creatures were killed. In 2002 the tanker *Prestige* sank off the coast of north-west Spain, after spilling about 27,000 tonnes of oil. To make things worse, it also took about 50,000 tonnes of oil down to the **seabed**. This may leak on to nearby beaches for years to come. See pages 28–29 for information on other major oil spills.

The map below shows the area affected by the Exxon Valdez *oil spill in 1989.*

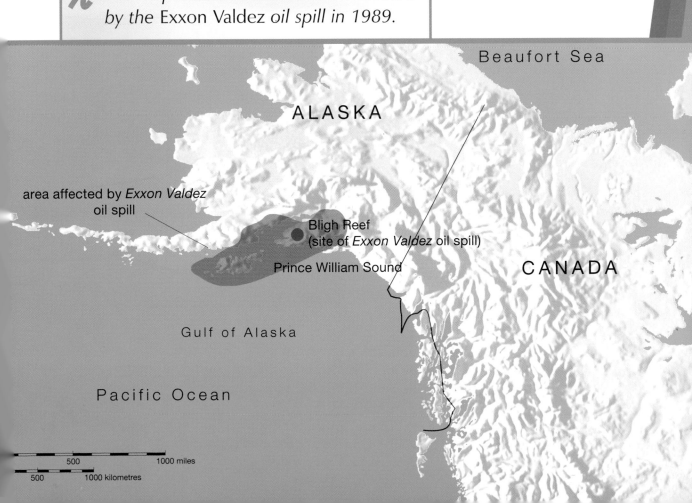

Beaufort Sea

ALASKA

area affected by *Exxon Valdez* oil spill

Bligh Reef (site of *Exxon Valdez* oil spill)

Prince William Sound

CANADA

Gulf of Alaska

Pacific Ocean

500   1000 miles
500   1000 kilometres

Rising sea levels

If sea levels were to rise around the globe, coastlines would be flooded all over the world. Ice at the North and South Poles is melting, because the global temperature is rising. Many scientists believe that this is caused partly by the **greenhouse effect**, which is created by heat-trapping gases. These allow heat through to Earth from the Sun, but trap it there, like the glass of a greenhouse. The gases we release by burning fuel, such as the exhaust fumes given off by cars, add to this effect. It may cause a general increase in temperature, called **global warming**, which would cause terrible problems to our coasts. A great deal of land would be flooded, including major cities such as London and New York.

Countries with low-lying coasts, such as the Netherlands, would suffer most from any rise in sea level. This large dam, 2.8 kilometres (1.7 miles) long, was built to stop flooding along a section of the Dutch coast.

Protecting our coasts

One of the problems for coasts is that they are so popular with people! This puts extra pressure on governments to protect coasts by turning coastlines into protected areas. Otherwise they would soon be ruined for everyone by **overdevelopment**.

National and marine parks

In many parts of the world, large areas of coast are being turned into national parks. In Florida, USA, Biscayne National Park (see map on page 23) is made up of protected islands, reefs and coastal waters. In Britain, the Pembrokeshire coast of west Wales is one of the country's official national parks. Nearly 600 square kilometres (232 square miles) of land is protected, and visitors can walk along almost the whole coastline. It is a favourite place for birdwatchers.

Looking to the future

Coastlines go on changing naturally over long periods of time. In recent years, many areas of coast have also changed dramatically because of the way in which people have treated them. Some of these changes have been good, but others have spoiled the regions' natural beauty. Accidents such as oil spills do great damage, and many people believe that our coasts should be even more protected.

Great Barrier Reef

The largest marine park in the world covers nearly 2000 kilometres (1250 miles) of the Great Barrier Reef, off the coast of Queensland, Australia. The park was created in the 1970s to protect the **coral** reefs, as well as the surrounding islands and coastline. On the local beaches there, as in other parts of the world, the motto is: 'Take nothing away and leave nothing but footprints'.

Coast facts and figures

Worst oil-tanker spills

tanker	location	year	spillage in thousands of tonnes
Atlantic Empress/ Aegean Captain	Trinidad	1979	300
Castillo de Bellver	Cape Town, S.Africa	1983	255
Olympic Bravery	Ushant, France	1976	250
Showa-Maru	Malacca, Malaysia	1975	237
Amoco Cadiz	Finistère, France	1978	223
Odyssey	Atlantic, off Canada	1988	140
Torrey Canyon	Scilly, UK	1967	120
Sea Star	Gulf of Oman	1972	115
Irenes Serenada	Pilos, Greece	1980	102
Urquiola	La Coruña, Spain	1976	101
Prestige	Galicia, Spain	2002	77

World's major ports

port	country	goods per year in millions of tonnes
Rotterdam	Netherlands	350
Singapore	Singapore	290
Chiba	Japan	174
Kobe	Japan	171
Hong Kong	China	147
Houston	USA	142
Shanghai	China	140
Nagoya	Japan	137
Yokohama	Japan	128
Antwerp	Belgium	110

The port of Rotterdam, in the Netherlands, is the busiest port in the world.

Countries with the longest coastlines

country	length in km	length in miles
Canada	244,800	152,112
Russia	103,000	64,002
Indonesia	40,000	24,855
Australia	36,735	22,826
Japan	33,287	20,684
Norway	21,347	13,264
USA	19,924	12,380
China	18,500	11,495

Most deadly tsunamis

location	year	estimated number of people killed
Lisbon, Portugal	1755	60,000
East Indies	1883	36,000
Japan	1707	30,000
Italy	1783	30,000
Japan	1896	27,000
Chile	1868	25,000
Ryukyu Islands	1771	12,000
Japan	1792	10,000
Philippines	1976	8000
Japan	1498	5000

This damage on the island of Okushiri was caused by a huge tsunami on 12 July 1993.

Glossary

abrasion process in which rocks are worn away by being hit and scraped by pebbles and stones

adapt change in order to suit the conditions

bar (or spit) long, narrow bank of sand that juts out into the sea from a sandy coast

bay wide, inward-curving part of the coast

boulder large stone that has been worn smooth

breaker sea wave that spills over and breaks into white foam on the shore

breakwater barrier of large boulders or concrete built out into the sea, which protects the coast by breaking up the force of waves

chalk white, soft kind of limestone rock

cliff steep rock face at the edge of the sea

climate weather conditions in a particular area

colony large group of animals, plants or people that live close together. A human colony is a settlement.

continent one of the world's seven huge land masses

coral tiny sea animal that forms colonies (called coral reefs) in warm, shallow waters

cove small bay

earthquake sudden shaking of the ground caused by movements beneath Earth's surface

erosion wearing away (especially rocks)

fjord long, narrow, deep inlet of the sea between high cliffs

glacier slowly moving mass of ice

global warming rise in temperature all over the world

granite very hard kind of rock, often used as a building stone

greenhouse effect trapping of the Sun's warmth near Earth by gases in the air

groyne wooden fence on a beach that stretches into the sea to break up waves and hold sand and pebbles in place

habitat natural environment, or home, of an animal or a plant

harbour place on the coast where ships come inland and shelter because it is protected from rough seas

headland piece of high land at the coast that juts out into the sea

health hazard something harmful that can cause illness

ice age period of time in the past when Earth was colder and more covered in ice

inlet thin strip of water extending from the sea into the land

lagoon stretch of water separated from the sea by a sandbank

marine animal animal that lives in the sea

mineral natural solid substance that is found in Earth's surface

overdevelopment too much building of houses and other developments in a place

peninsula piece of land that is almost surrounded by water

pollute damage with harmful substances

predator animal that hunts and kills other animals for food

resort place that is popular for holidays

sea anemone sea animal with stinging tentacles

seabed ground under the sea; the ocean floor

settlement place where people live permanently

sewage human waste matter

shellfish sea creature with a shell, such as an oyster or a crab

shore land along the edge of the sea

spit (or bar) long, narrow bank of sand that juts out into the sea from a sandy coast

strata layers of rock

tsunami giant wave caused by an earthquake or erupting volcano

valley low area between mountains

volcanic rock rock formed when the lava thrown out by a volcano hardens

waterline level reached by the sea on a beach or cliff

Further reading

Amazing Journeys: Along the Seashore, Rod Theodorou and Carole Telford (Heinemann Library, 2001)

Coasts and Islands, Terry Jennings (Belitha Press, 1999)

Earth Alert: Coasts, John Baines (Hodder Wayland, 2001)

Earth in danger: Coasts, Polly Goodman (Hodder Wayland, 2001)

Eyewitness Guides: Seashore, Steve Parker (Dorling Kindersley, 1989)

The Coast Book, Brian Knapp (Atlantic Europe Publishing Co Ltd, 2002)

The Natural World: Bustling Coastlines, Barbara Taylor (Ticktock Media, 2000)

Index